Blacky
the Black Snake

By Julia Poirot Thoma

Illustrated by
Susan Raymond

Grampa always referred to himself as "Just a plain old dirt farmer." He loved dirt and spent his whole life studying it and all the things that grow in it.

PRAIRIE GRASS

He often talked about how all the food we eat and most of the clothes we wear come from things that grow in the dirt.

He understood well how
life on earth worked.
He loved all critters,
from the smallest
insect to the biggest bear.

He even wrote a book about how the
smallest and weakest ones are eaten
by the larger ones. Insects eat plants
and nectar; small animals eat plants
and insects and worms. Then larger
animals eat plants, small animals,
and even other large animals.

Many such critters lived near
Grampa's house on the prairie.
There were rabbits, skunks, mice,
rats, many many different kinds
of birds and one big black snake.

Now, almost everyone loves
furry bunnies and fuzzy
baby birds, but Grampa
loved all of nature's
creatures—even Blacky,
the slithery black snake.
Blacky was about three
feet long and as big
around as a chocolate
chip cookie.

Blacky might be found
sunning on the back step
or stretched out on a
shady branch of the big
old elm tree. On cold
winter days, he curled
up behind a tool box
or wrapped himself
around a warm pipe in
the basement. Sometimes,
as he got bigger, he would
slide right out of his skin.
Next morning there it
would be, wrapped
around the pipe.

Blacky feasted on
mice and rats
in the shed

where Grampa stored hay
and turkey feed.

Once he ate all the baby wrens
right out of their nest as
Grandma watched in horror.

"Everything eats
something smaller and
weaker," Grampa opined.
"Too bad it was the
baby birds this time."

One day a young man
was visiting. He had a
new gun and asked
Grampa, "Is it okay if I
shoot tin cans off the
back fence posts?"
"Sure, just be careful
you don't shoot toward
any of the buildings,"
Grampa cautioned.

Unfortunately, it was a hot day.

Blacky was sleeping on a
shady limb up in the elm tree.

The young man aimed, pulled the
trigger and shot Blacky dead. He
didn't understand that Blacky was a
helpful snake who ate the rats and
mice that ate the turkey feed.

The young man proudly presented the dead snake to Grampa on the end of a very long stick.

Grampa got very quiet. With sad eyes, he looked at Blacky and then at the young man. Grampa was sad because of the senseless death, but he understood that the young man, like many people, thought the snake was dangerous. So, he said, "Well, that's all right. Just don't shoot any other living thing without asking me first."

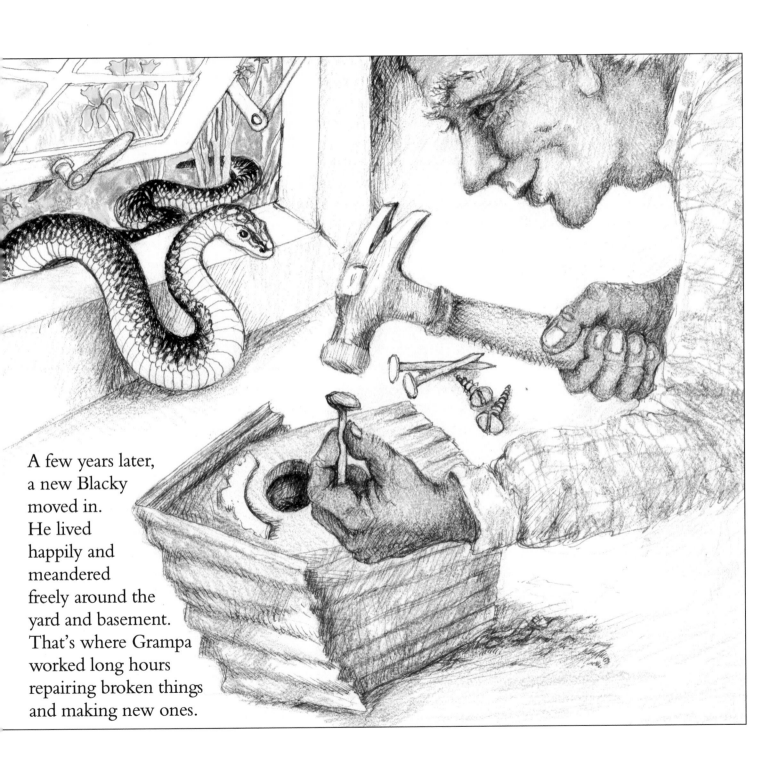

A few years later, a new Blacky moved in. He lived happily and meandered freely around the yard and basement. That's where Grampa worked long hours repairing broken things and making new ones.

Grampa and Grandma lived happily on the farm for many years. Grampa was almost ninety years old when he died. He wrote in his book that God created death so that there could be new life. Seeds die so sprouts can grow. Animals and plants die to give their nutrients back to the soil, so new plants will have food to grow. "So too, people must die," he would say, "or else there would be so many people, we would eat up all the food and fill up all the space on Earth."

"God created death so that there could be new life"

BLACKY I

Grandma continued living in the old farm house and so did Blacky. Grandma also loved the prairie flowers and animals.

She especially loved the spring mornings when all the birds sang to awaken her. She wasn't quite so fond of Blacky, but she knew how much Grampa liked him, so she let him stay in the yard.

Blacky must have missed Grampa because he moved upstairs where Grandma spent most of her days. She was frequently startled to see him stretched out under the dining table, curled up under the sink or on the stairs. Picking up the phone she often called her son who lived up the road a little way.

"Son, would you please come and put Blacky back in the basement?"

One day the cleaning lady opened the washer to see if the clothes were finished. There was Blacky swishing around in the suds with the sheets.

"Eeeeeeeek," she screamed and she fainted right there on the kitchen floor. Grandma calmly called her son. "Please come and put Blacky back in the yard before he drowns."

A few years later Grandma also died. After a glorious celebration of her long life with song and feasting, all the children and grandchildren gathered at the old farm house. Each one got to take some of their most favorite things. Some chose dishes, tools, chairs, vases or napkins.

One grandson wanted Grampa's big old bureau. He loaded it onto a truck and after everyone said goodbye, he took it to his home in a nearby town.

A couple days later, he opened the top drawer to put his things in it. There was Blacky sleeping in the corner with Grampa's underwear and socks. "Oh, Blacky, you'd be happier back on the farm."

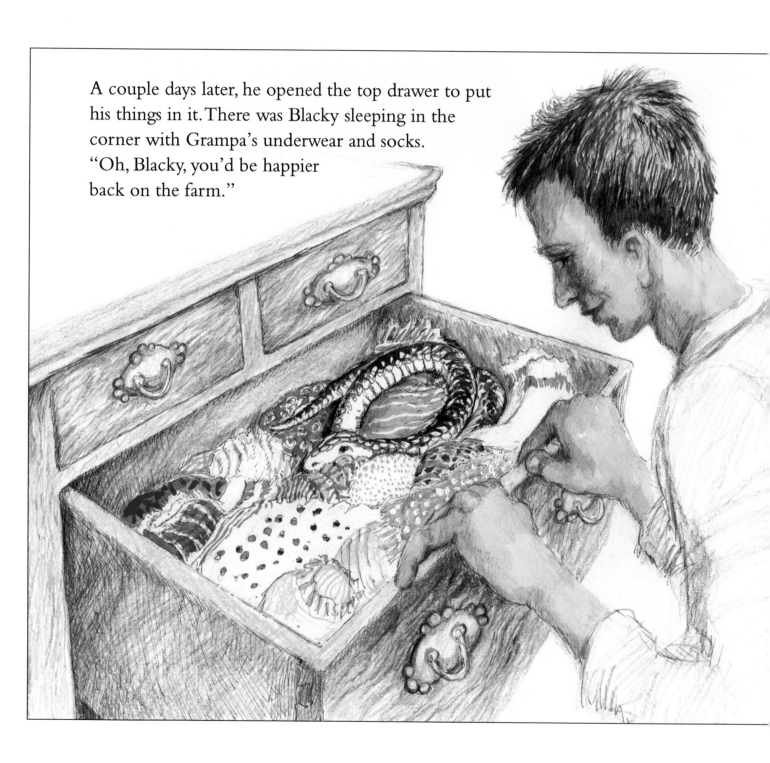

The grandson carefully put Blacky
in a cardboard box
and carried him back to the prairie.

Author's Notes

The author's parents, Eugene and May Poirot, were the
inspiration for the characters Grampa and Grandma in
this book. Eugene and May graduated together from
the University of Illinois in 1922. Eugene authored *Our
Margin of Life* and *Permission to Life*, which chronicled his
research and experiences farming. May Frances Brady Poirot wrote
stories and poems in her later life for the enjoyment of her children and
grandchildren. They lived out their lives on a farm in southwest Missouri.
The farm continues to be worked by their son and his family. A portion
of the acreage is prairie land. This land, never having been plowed,
supports many grasses and plants found only in virgin
prairies.

About Snakes

Many different kinds of snakes are black, and some
are poisonous. Blacky was a nonpoisonous Black
Rat Snake. Black Rat Snakes live in a broad
swath of the midwestern and southern United
States. They eat rodents, birds, and bird eggs.
Even though Grampa and his grandson picked
up Blacky to move him to some other location,
no one should ever pick up a snake unless they have
been taught how to distinguish between poisonous
and nonpoisonous ones.

LIMBERTWIG PRESS
Fayetteville, Arkansas

ISBN-13: 978-0-9841314-2-6

BOOK DESIGN: Liz Lester Design
(www.lizlesterdesign.com)

Limbertwig Press

Small books, big heart.

P.O. Box 758
Farmington, AR 72730-0758
479-582-1092
www.limbertwig.us

LaVergne, TN USA
13 August 2010
193190LV00002B